# The Children of Hope

## For a United World

Canada
Colombia
D. R. Congo
Brazil

Pakistan
India
Philippines
Malawi

# The Children of Hope

For a United World

'The Work is published with the support of the Publication
Assistance Programmes of the Institut français'

PAP
TAGORE

This edition was published by arrangement with The Picture Book Agency, France.

**First Edition :** 2023



ISBN : 978-93-92088-26-1

**Price:** ₹ 349

**Published by**
**Unbound Script**
B-10, Seven Wonder Business Center
Plot No. G-20, Basement, Preet Vihar
New Delhi-110092
**E-mail :** books@unboundscript.com
**Website :**www.unboundscript.com

**Printed in India**

**THE CHILDREN OF HOPE**: For a United World
by Annick De Giry & Bruno Pilorget

*Translated by* Prachi Agarwal

# The Children of Hope

## For a United World

Annick De Giry, Bruno Pilorget

Translation
**Prachi Agarwal**

UNBOUND SCRIPT

# Contents

# Introduction

For millions of kids, growing up is a journey fraught with hardships and future an unattainable dream. Still few do not let their hope wither. From Philippines to Pakistan and India, from Tanzania to Brazil and Colombia, from Malawi to Canada, these are battles of 8 kids from amongst many others.

From a very small age they faced difficult situations, many a times inhuman but they overcame their fears, exhaustion, discouragement and sufferance and used it as a springboard trampoline so as to motivate other kids. Their age did not stop them from assuming responsibility of changing their lives and to make the world respect their rights.

## Declaration of the Rights of the Child

In 1959, The United Nations adopted the Declaration of Rights of the Child applicable on every child irrespective of their nationality, religion or colour. These are the right to a name and nationality; right to proper nourishment, home and care; right to education and special care in case of an handicap; right to love, affection and joy; right to protection against danger and exploitation; the child be taught tolerance, solidarity and friendship amongst people. The nations signing this declaration pledge to vote laws for respect of children's rights.

"Pens and books are the strongest weapons against terrorism"

# MALALA—Fighting for girl education

**Name** : Malala Yousafzai

**Birth** : 12 July, 1997 in the region of Swat, north west Pakistan

**Nationality** : Pakistani

**Book** : I am Malala–the girl who stood up for education and was shot by Talibans

**International Peace Prize for Children**

**Sakharov Prize**

**Nobel Peace Prize**

Malala and her family lived in the Swat valley, a beautiful region in the north west of Pakistan. High mountains overlooked the prairies, forests and the little lakes. The people of the valley however lived in constant terror: since 2007, the talibans who came from the neighbouring country of Afganistan, made the valley their hideout and terrorized its people who were forced to follow an extremist religion where women did not have the right to a free life. Whoever opposed them was put to death. In such extreme situations even the army was unable to exercise its power.

At the risk of her life, Malala decided to raise her voice against the talibans and to fight for the right of girls to go to school.

## 2008-2009

**The diary of a Pakistani school student**

Malala was 11 years old and she loved studying and going to school but life was never same again after the talibans tookover the valley. In her blog that she wrote under a pen-name, she described her school life.

**14 January 2009:** "This time the girls were not excited about the vacations because they knew that if the talibani decree is imposed in the valley, they will never be able to return to school."

"I realized the importance of school when it was forbidden in Swat. Why did no one dare to speak against the atrocities committed on us?"

In fact the talibans demanded the closure of girl's schools from February and worse still, they ransacked and destroyed more that 150 academic institutions!

As more and more readers joined Malala's blog, her success troubled the talibans; despite her pen name, they identified her and started threatening her. Every night before going to sleep she checked all the doors in her house but she did not give up writing. Her parents encouraged her to write–after all the talibans will not dare attack a kid!

## May-July 2009: Exile

Malala admired her father; he was one of those few men who dared to speak against the talibans. However, the day when a video was circulated showing some of them frisking a

young girl in public, the entire valley reacted: this time it was just too much.

The army attacked the talibans and soon life looked impossible amidst gun shots and explosions. Like many other inhabitants, Malala's family had to leave the valley leaving everything behind them: books, chicken...

A few months later when the talibans were chased out of the valley and peace returned, people started returning back home.

## Returning Home

Excited, Malala's brothers ran inside their house to find their hens but the grains they had left were not enough and they did not survive. As for Malala, she went straight to her room. Full of books, her school bag was lying as she had left it. Nothing was missing. Her father's school was almost intact and Malala could once more go back to school. Her life normalized...untill that fatidic day in October 2012.

## 9 October 2012, The Assault

Malala was 15 years old. That day they were 15 girls who boarded the school bus to go back home after school. The moment the bus started, two men barged in:

"Which one of you is Malala?"

Terrorised, the girls turned towards the only girl who was not wearing a veil. Shot, the three injured girls collapsed while the two men fled.

Malala was seriously injured on the head and the shoulder and went into coma. She was operated in emergency but her condition remained critical. She would die if she was not shifted to a better equipped hospital. Few days later, she was transported by an air ambulance to a super speciality hospital for war injuries in Birmingham, England.

## February 2013: Birmingham

For the first time after the attack, when Malala looked at herself in the mirror, she was shocked. The entire left side of her face was paralysed. It would take time for her to be like before or almost... But her purpose summoned her. Her family joined her in England and she was flocked with messages from all over the world.

## Recognition for her foundation

Even though she almost lost her life, she was more than ever convinced about her fight. Every meeting, every school visit, every library inauguration was an occasion for her to strengthen her conviction: everywhere in the world, girls should have access to education.

In 2013, on her 16th birthday, she was invited to the United Nations meet where she reminded hundreds of youth present there that education is a right of every child:

" I speak on behalf of all those who fight for their right to live in peace, their right to dignity and equal chances and their right to education."

Her relentless fight got her numerous recognitions. At the age of 17, she became the youngest noble peace price laureate and all the rewards allowed her to strengthen her foundation that she established to fight for education of girls.

Despite being threatened by talibans who warned that the next time she would not survive, she increased her public appearances. Her book, I am Malala, is a proof of her determination.

She dreams of becoming the Prime Minister to be able to change the Pakistani society. Her courage has made her an icon amongst the youth.

## Education–a Priority

The talibans were chased out of Pakistan only to come back. The girls once again became the target of their attacks. If the education of girls has become such a big issue in a country deprived of freedom, it is because the number of girls in the schools is much less than that of boys. Yet Malala is convinced that in all societies it is only women who can transform existing mentalities.

“One is never too small to help others”

# KESZ—Helping roadside kids

**Name** : Cris Valdez, known name – Kesz

**Birth** : 26 December, 1998 in Cavite, Philippines

**Nationality** : Philipini

International Peace prize for children

Scattered like confetti on the Pacific Ocean in the south west of China, thousands of islands together constitute Philippines—the archipelago regularly swept by thunders and typhoons. It's economic progress in the last few years is marred by undying poverty. Close to 25,000 kids live on the roads. In the outskirts of Cavite, some 30 kms from Manilla, Kesz, a kid raised on the road, decided to turn his life around.

## Life in the slum

A man emerged from a hut hustling a kid along him:

"Out! Get lost! And don't dare come back without any money!"

Scared, Kesz ran away to join the other kids like him on the landfill next to the slum.

This was how it had been since he was a small baby. His father would beat him and force him to beg and rummage the garbage for any thing that he could sell to buy alcohol and drugs. His mother never tried to save him. When he was small, his parents tried to sell him off but in vain. Ever since they believed that Kesz was unlucky for them.

## The Landfill

A big truck, passed by the kids blowing its horn loudly and stopped a little way ahead to dump the garbage. Kesz and a dozen other kids, some bare feet, rushed to climb up the garbage mound. They frantically rummaged the trash looking to gather anything worth a few cents—plastic bottles, tin cans, metal pieces—hoping miraculously to find a valuable object thrown by mistake which they could sell for a fortune.

Kesz was only 4 and he couldn't take it anymore. He then decided never to return back home. He spent the day begging or on the landfill and at night he slept under a shop's

porch or in the cemetery. He and his friends had found empty graves where they could hide in the rain.

## The Accident

One evening, a pile of tires was burning in the corner of the landfill. As soon as the last garbage truck emptied itself, the kids ran up pushing each other. Kesz lost his balance as they rushed up the landfill.

"Carefull!" shouted a boy

Too late though! Kesz fell in the flames and his clothes caught fire. His back and arms were severely burnt and he suffered terribly. Since a year and a half, he had not gone back home but now he had no choice but to return to his parent's house.

"Couldn't you be more careful? Don't think that I will pay for your treatment", shouted his father!

Fortunately, his mother knew who could help them: Manalaysay, a social worker who often roamed in the streets of the slum. In the club that he set up for them kids, he offered activities and games for kids as a way to save them from gangs that looked to take them in. Well aware of the life Kesz was leading, he agreed to take care of him and to keep him in a children's shelter till the time he would get well again.

## A new life

After a few months, Kesz's mother came knocking at his door. She had not come to ask about her son, instead she said to him, "me and my husband, we do not want Kesz back. He is of no use to us."

Manalaysay could not bring himself to abandon the child. He leaned towards him and said, "don't worry, I will take care of you."

The only way was to adopt him. It was a long procedure but he finally got the permission. For the first time in life, Kesz felt loved and he could go to school also. Slowly he wanted to live again.

Kesz did not know his exact age. After searching for long, he finally found out that he was born on 26th December 1998 and the day he turned 7 he celebrated his birthday for the first time. He couldn't believe it–candles, cake, gifts! He was a little disoriented and only thought of sharing all that he had got with his friends whom he had not forgotten.

## Gifts of hope

Kesz made little parcels and distributed them amongst the children on the roads. He called them the "gifts of hope". He so wanted that his friends gather courage like him but soon he had nothing to give away.

He then found local shopkeepers and asked them to give him some confectionaries and

slippers for his parcels. Most of the kids on the roads roamed bare feet and often got hurt at the landfill. His guardian supported him:

—What if you created an association? It would be a good way to get donations and help from others, he suggested.

With his friends and other kids of the school, he soon set up a committee to support the kids on the road. They could be recognized in their yellow t-shirts. One of the groups collected shoes, sweets, clothes, toothbrushes, soaps, toys...another group sorted and packed them and yet another distributed the parcels.

Every week after class, Kesz and his team gathered together the kids on the roads and explained to them how to wash their hands, brush their teeth, clean their wounds. Those who understood, taught other kids.

## Changing the world

Kesz overcame his difficult past and in a few years he changed the lives of thousands of kids who, like him, were victim of child abuse and violence. In 2012, at the age of 12, he was bestowed with the international peace prize for kids.

Raising his trophy, he said, "my message to the children from all over the world is that they should never lose hope."

## Prize

This prize allowed him to continue his work for the kids on the roads and also to pursue his studies. He wanted to be a doctor.

### International Peace Prize for Kids

In 2005, a Dutch association, Kidsrights, created the international peace prize for kids. It is equivalent of the Nobel peace prize but for kids. Nkosi, a young south African suffering from AIDS by birth, fought during the 12 years of his life so that others suffering from this viral disease be accepted in the society. His story was so inspiring that he became the first laureate of this prize posthumously.

Since then, every year, a kid braving particularly difficult circumstances and who helps others caught in similar situations is chosen from all over the world for the prize. This prize is meant to help them continue their mission. The trophy, named Nkosi in honour of the young south African kid, represents a kid holding out a sphere in front of him: **even a kid can change the world.**

"Family is the strongest support to face the challenges of life."

# SANDRA–Changing the slums

| | |
|---|---|
| **Name** | : Sandra Liliana Sanchez |
| **Birth** | : 28 May, 1985 South Bogata, Columbia |
| **Nationality** | : Columbian |
| **Book** | : Les oubliés de Bogata (The forgottens of Bogata) |

In the last forty years, Colombia is ravaged by the civil war with daily clashes between the government and the gorillas – the revolutionary army. The civilians, caught between the two, flee from the villages that have become dangerous to live only to take refuge in the slum of the capital city of Bogata, not knowing where else to go.

Sandra was 7 years old when she reached one of these miserable slums with her family. The shock for her was huge but overcoming the misery, she changed the life in the slum by kindling a sense of kinship amongst its inhabitants.

## From one paradise to another

Four silhouettes carrying bundles started walking on mud path leaving the paved road. A man carrying a small girl of 2, a pregnant woman and a little girl of 7 years walked for two hours to cross from north Bogata, the area of the rich, to south, the area of the slums. After another hour of climb the parents finally stopped.

"Here we are," said the father putting the small girl down.

"But where is the house?" asked the older Sandra.

"We are going to build it. Tonight we will have to stay under a plastic canvas. We will start work from tomorrow."

This was not possible; they won't live in a dirty place like this! Despite difficulties, Sandra had a happy childhood. Since her father had a lot of difficulties in finding a job, the family was staying with their grandfather. Sandra loved to hear him tell stories about their country and after school she played for hours with her cousins in the countryside. But their presence became a burden and they had to leave.

## Hell or Paradise

The slum where thay came to live was called 'El Paraiso'—The Paradise. Sandra was terrified to be surrounded by the chaotic construction–

houses built out of bamboo and plastic canvas or of brick and corrugated iron sheets for those who were a little less poor. The ground and streets were strewn with dust and garbage. There was neither electricity nor running water.

Water was the biggest challenge. People had to fetch it from a stream a kilometer away. As for school, it was four brick walls with plastic sheets as windows and two room without electricity filled with 200 kids. Very often the kids gave up their classes after a few months for a small work on the road. Earning a few cents was always better than having nothing. Sandra missed her lovely school in the village.

## At El Paraiso, we don't give away our share of bread

During the break, the little girl watched her classmates playing football. She unwraped her

sandwich and threw the wrapper on the ground –in El Paraiso, there were no dustbins. A boy saw her, came running and licked the crumbs stuck on the paper and went back to play. After the class, Sandra went to talk to him:

"Why didn't you ask me for the sandwich?"

"Because you would have given it to me, perhaps?"

"Of course", I had two slices!

"At El Paraiso, we never give our bread", he replied.

## Action at 9

This statement jolted her like electric current. Suddenly Sandra's opinion about her classmates changed. This boy, his eyes betrayed starvation, a look that cannot be missed by someone who knew hunger well. He does not even have a note-book to write in. The decision was taken, she will fight it: the need was to create a sense of solidarity rather than each one fighting alone for oneself. In a few months, Sandra was so well known in her school that she became an elected representative of her school and worked as an intermediary between her school and the government. She was only 9? How does it matter: she wrote to the administration, found officials and very soon the result could be seen. The school got actual doors and windows, running water, more teachers and computers also! With the help of the mayor, she organised fates, academic aid and even Christmas gifts for little kids...

## Bridging generations

One afternoon, while returning from class, Sandra noticed an old lady sitting at a counter.

She was petite, decked in a cap, a thick pair of glasses, carrying a stick. Margarita waited patiently that some of her neighbours put together a shelter for her. Sandra decided to go talk to her. In a few days they become friends and then on a Friday evening Sandra has an idea:

"Margarita, do you want to come over for dinner with us?" she asked her.

Returning back after dinner "with family" that evening, Margarita hugged Sandra:

"You can't imagine how happy I am this evening, little Sandra. I wish it is Friday every day."

It was a revelation for Sandra. This was her mission at El Paraiso: create a link between the elderly people, who had no one to talk to all day long, and the disoriented youth.

Since then, every Friday, Margarita invited other elderly people like her and the kids joined in also. Gradually Sandra discovered the distress of the older people abandoned by their families. Soon her parent's house became too small for the Friday reunion. It was a new challenge but two years later, the Oasis – a community house– came into existence. With one meal served daily, everyone talked, narrated stories, played music. The elderly transmitted their knowledge to the young while the latter rekindled their zeal in life.

## Education for action

Sandra found some people to continue her work so that she could focus on her studies which was her priority. She wanted to become a lawyer to be able to defend the poor.

### The most important is Solidarity

El Paraiso has transformed drastically with time and its inhabitants lead a more dignified life. But Sandra was worried because material progress overshadowed the solidarity. Moreover the problem of displaced families remained unresolved. When they arrive in the slum, they are not accepted. The parents want to go back to their farms in their villages. The kids however want to stay back despite the fear of exclusion, insecurity, risk of forced recruitment by gangs. However, like Sandra, some of the youth are motivated to join politics and change the views of people around them.

" I understood that people tried to save my childhood that was being destroyed by my own family"

# OM—Liberating slave Kids

**Nom** : Om Prakash Gurjar

**Birth** : 3 July, 1992 in the village of Rajasthan, India

**Nationality** : Indian

**International Children's Peace Prize**

Rajasthan in the north west of India is a city of maharajas and incredible richesse that attracts thousands of tourists. Its reality however is not so promising. All around in the fields, farms, workshops, cement factories, textile and carpet mills, we come across children working for meager salaries. Some are not even paid. These are slave child labourers. The mill and factory owners exploit them for their profits.

Om was also one of them. Since the age of 5, he worked in a farm. Liberated at 8, he then went to school and started his battle: liberating the slave kids.

"Om, we met your parents and the owner. This is it and now you are free!"

The child, hunched over the ground, looked up. He knew the man who came to give him this unbelievable news. Free? How was that possible?

## Slave kids

Om was a slave kids like many other. One day when he was all of 5, someone came to his parent's house to take him to the farm. That day onwards, from morning to evening, with only two meals a day, he looked after the farm animals, sowing and harvest and was beaten at the smallest of errors. Nobody ever told him that his father, an agricultural labourer, had taken money from his land lord and to repay the debt, he had to pledge himself and his children to his service without being paid in return. This truly was slavery.

## Freedom

Om had been working in the farm for three years when a man went upto his parents,

"Your son is very small to work and he is not even paid!" Do you know that child labour

is against the law? He should return here and go to school.

The social worker belonged to the association Save the Kids. He went round the country trying to liberate the slave kids.

" It is impossible", said his father. " I still owe a lot of money to the landlord for whom he works. He will be furious if Om came back"

This did not deter the social worker's determination. He returned to persuade his parents and the landlord. After long discussions, they finally agreed to free the child. The association volunteered to take care of his education.

## Bal Ashram

Om entered a Bal Ashram, a house for the victims of abuse and exploitation. They stayed there for a few months or a few years to get education and to regain their confidence. Om went on to become the representative of the children's association. Once in 6 months he returned home to meet his parents and his 6 brothers and sisters.

## Free Schooling

The kid was eager to start learning but the government school where he wanted to study asked his parents for 100 rupees for his books and school fee. But this was against the law because in India, public schools were free. The young boy approached a lawyer:

"Is it not wrong for the school to ask my parents for money?"

"You are right, Om, said the lawyer. The school should give free education. Do you know other kids facing the same problem?"

"Many!"

"So this is what we are going to do: you will get a petition signed by all these kids which we will present in the Rajasthan court. The law has to be respected."

Two hundred kids of his school signed the petition and justice was delivered: school had to reimburse the parents. Om didn't stop here. He approached other schools and fought it out

with the management. The movement spread fast and then there was a day when none of the public schools in Rajasthan asked parents to pay for their child's admission. Om was very proud of his first victory.

## Ghost Kids

A lot of kids don't have birth certificate and thus do not exist for the state. These are the ghost kids and this is a big reason of their exploitation.

Om started registration camps and, in a few years, more than 500 girls and boys got this important certificate. This proof of their age would help protect them against slavery, child trafficking and forced marriage. This was just his second victory in his ongoing combats. But Om did not forget his beginning years and could not bear to see children working. With the help of volunteers of the association that had saved him, he took up the mammoth task of liberating them. At every point he came across indifferent officers who seemed to ignore the laws. Fortunately, he was able to set up a network of "villages –friends of children" where it was prohibited to make children work. He even managed to make his native village a part of this network. Now all his brothers and sisters could go to school.

His mission soon got a lot of recognisition and got him the international peace prize for children in 2006.

Om is now in his twenties. Along with his studies, he is pursuing his mission in India and in Nepal. His dream is to become the governor of his area to free all kids from slavery and build a world more aware of their rights.

## International Convention of children's rights

Many countries have recognized the 1959 declaration of the Rights of the child but do not impose its directives. Thirty years hence an international convention for children's rights is created. The countries signing this convention pledge to respect these rights and the protection of kids is supervised by a committee. In 1992, India signed this convention with one out of five kids living in India.

"Is it fair that we wake up to the sound of gun shots? Kids have a right to protection!"

# MAYRA–Fighting against Violence

**Name** : Mayra Avellar Neves

**Birth** : Sometime in 1991 in Favela de vila Cruzerio, Rio de Jenerio

**Nationality** : Brazilian

**International Peace Prize for children.**

Brazil is that one country in the world where the gap between rich and poor is the largest. One out of three persons lives in a favela-slums in the outskirts of cities. In these favelas many had jobs – bus or taxi drivers, house maids or police men/women—but they lived in miserable conditions. For the others, it was about making ends meets by hook or by crook, drugs and arms trafficking.

The favela in vila Cruzeiro, Rio de Janerio is one of the most dangerous in the country and this is where Mayra lived.

## Daily Violence

In lack of necessities and education, the risk of the youth getting involved in drug trafficking and crime increases manyfold. In these slums violence reigns over law and order. Life in the favela is not alone

miserable but impossible with violent clashes between the drug trafficking gangs firing on the policemen who try to dislodge them. Caught between the crossfire, the inhabitants hide in their houses. More than hundred youth got killed every year, hit by stray shots. As a homage to their lost children, families etched the names of their kids on the walls.

## Peace march

Mayra just turned 15 and the violence was at its peak in vila Cruzerio. The police had decided to launch a major operation "clean-up" of the traffickers. Barricades were put up; teachers and doctors from outside the slum could no longer enter and so all classes were called off.

Blocked inside her house, Mayra rebelled: she found it unfair that the students be forced to stay locked up in their houses because of the clashes between the gangs and the police. What if she organised a children's protest march? They had hardly started walking that other rushed to join the demonstration, despite the danger, as the entire procession has to pass by the heavily armed policemen. The march surprised everyone. The children won; the police agreed not to interfere during school hours; school could finally reopen.

Mayra understood the power of a protest march. In the following year, she organized a second protest march. More than three hundred people took part: adults, kids, slumdwellers and inhabitants of surrounding areas. They demanded equal rights for the inhabitants of the favela. It was a success yet again. The

government was forced to take action and install the basic equipment promised since long.

## One culture for all

Mayra knew that education was the only way to surmount the miserable conditions. She was also aware that education alone did not constitute culture, it is also art, cinema, theatre, danse, all that allows to think, to imagine and to believe in the possibility of another life.

In a small room in the favela, she set up a cinema where a film was projected once a month followed by a discussion. The spectators were mostly the young between the age of 15 and 18 never wanting to miss a show. The advantage of films is that everyone could understand it weather they knew to read and write or not.

Mayra joined a theatre troupe aswell and one day the organiser announced that a troupe from Netherlands had invited six young actors to participate in a show. There would also be dancers from Kenya, India and Ghana. For the first time the world was opening up for them.

## 17 years: meetings

Mayra's actions transformed the favela slowly and steadily and in 2008 she was chosen for the international children's peace prize. This reward was an opportunity to improve not only the film locale but the entire favela would benefit from it.

This reward changed the entire population's perception of the slum dwellers. The young brazilian met the education minister and the

Rio government. They pledged to improve the education for the whole country. She was also invited to participate in an international conference on development in Johannesburg, South Africa.

## University

Mayra's parents suggested that she leaves the favela to live somewhere else in the city but Mayra refused. She started studying History - a subject that she wanted to teach later. According to her it is only in remembering the past that one can avoid repeating the same errors and move ahead.

### Footballl, Joy and Misery

The Brazilians were very proud: their country had been chosen to host the 2014 football world cup and the 2016 Olympic games. Elsewhere, it was primordial that the drug traffickers of the favela be dislodged. Everything was planned- troupes, helicopters and tanks.....People were witness to real war scenes. Today the roads are quieter than before but something much bigger than a military action was required for the situation to change considerably. A lot of Brazilians were scandalized at the huge amounts being spent on sport equipment when many lacked the basic necessities. In what capacity were these events beneficial for the Brazilians as a whole?

“Growing up in a refugee camp was like growing up to no future.”

# BARUANI—Giving voice to the refugee kids!

**Name** : Baruani Ndume

**Birth** : Around 1993, in Congo

**Nationality** : Cogolese

**International peace prize for Children**

Zaire, Belgian-Congo, Congo-Kinshasa, Democratic Republic of Congo (DRC), the successive names of the same country stand proof of its tumultuous history. Sitting at the heart of Africa, it suffered endlessly the repercussions of the conflicts in its neighbourhood. As for the Congolese themselves, they were continuously fighting among themselves. Fear reigned all over.

Baruani was born in this country incessantly ravaged by wars. At the age of 7 he lost everything: his house, his family. In the refugee camp where he lived thereafter, he understood the importance of speaking about his pain and suffering to get over them. Through Radio Espoire (Hope Radio), he was able to give voice to other refugee kids aswell.

## The Escape

1998, in the region of South Kivu in DRC, a terrorised Baruani ran away. At the age of 7, he experienced the most horrible event of his life. Soldiers entered his village, he and his mother were locked with other inhabitants in a house before it was put on fire. As he was small, he was able to slip through a small opening and saved himself. He ran from there and a old lady who was also able to escape from the village took charge of him.

After a long unending walk, they could see the Lake Tanganyika from far. At the other side, the refugee camps in Tanzania greeted those who escaped violence in their country. The tired kid and the old lady had no choice but to stay in one of the camps.

## Refugee Camps

Baruani couldn't get over the shock of losing his entire family. He had to live in the camp that he hardly knew.

He was getting used to the camp when the old lady decided to leave the camp for another to live with her daughter and took him with her.

The new camp was rather dangerous. In the name of a camp there were kilometers of shelters lined up without a safe corner, rout with poverty. The orphaned kids were lodged with guardians who often illtreated and exploited them. The food ration that was distributed once in a month was grossly insufficient.

The kids in the camp had all gone through traumatic situations. Some had seen their parents assassinated in front of their eyes while some others were separated from them during the attacks. They were all terrified and felt abandoned

without friends or family. Such was the case of Baruani also. The old lady left him in the care of her daughter who beat him and refused to give him food or clothes. She forced him to transport heavy bundles of wood (heavier than he could lift). He endured everything silently as he was completely helpless but all this took a toll on his health and he would not even have the energy to go to the school in the camp.

One day, volunteers from an association came to speak to the kids about their rights. Baruani realised that he had to react even though it was difficult to speak about all that he endured every day. He couldn't let this chance go by. The volunteers decided to speak to his guardian and explained to her that she did not have the right to ill treat him like she did. From that day life became a little easy for Baruani.

## Radio Espoire : Radio Hope

Baruani was much better and began taking interest in all that was going on around him. In the camp a parliament of kids tried to resolve their problems and when the need arose to elect a representative of the kids, Baruani presented himself and was chosen. For the first time in his life Baruani was filled with a sense of pride.

What was still required was that their voice be heard. The young boy was going to make it possible. A decade ago, to help the survivors of the civil war and the massacres in the neighbouring countries, the Jesuits –the Catholics– launched Radio Kwizera which means Radio Espoire or Radio Hope. Soon a program presented by the kids was reserved for them. Yet again Baruani was chosen to take responsibility. The team of journalists gave him the material and explained him how to go about it.

"Kids for Kids" This was the name of their program. Baruani gathered all the young reporters and sent them across the camp to interrogate other kids on their problems and difficulties:

"My parents force me to get water every day. The cans become very heavy when full. There after I do not have the energy to attend classes."

"When we came to class there were neither tables nor chairs. We had to make them ourselves. More over none of us had notebooks or pencils."

"Me too, I am too tired to go to class. My guardian receives food on my name but he prefers to sell it to earn a little money"

R.D.CONGO

Baruani knew how painful it can be to keep your suffering bottled up inside you. He had experienced it himself. When they expressed themselves in public, kids gained in confidence and come out with solutions to better their lives.

The little reporters returned to office and discussed the problems narrated. After recording the narratives, they sent the cassettes to the local radio who broadcast it.

## Success of Radio Kwizera

On a Sunday afternoon, when Baruani was roaming in the camp, he noticed a lot of people gathered around those with a radio. It was the time his program was aired. He had not imagined such a huge success. Slowly the attitude of adults also changed.

The radio made miracles possible: the kids came to the mike to tell their names, the name of their village and their story. They appealed to their friends and family members who might be listening to them. Thanks to the program, many kids were reunited with their lost families.

## Recognition

By the time he turned 16, Baruani had been able to bring about such a change in the life of the kids in the camp that he was chosen for the international peace prize for children.

Sometime later, he went to attend a conference in Johannesburg in South Africa focusing on the betterment of human rights. There he met Mayra who was also invited to the conference. His English had improved tremendously and he no longer required an interpretor to speak.

He continues to run the radio program and it fascinates him so much that he wishes to go to the university one day and become a well-known journalist. To his mind, it is the best way to spread awareness across the globe about children's rights.

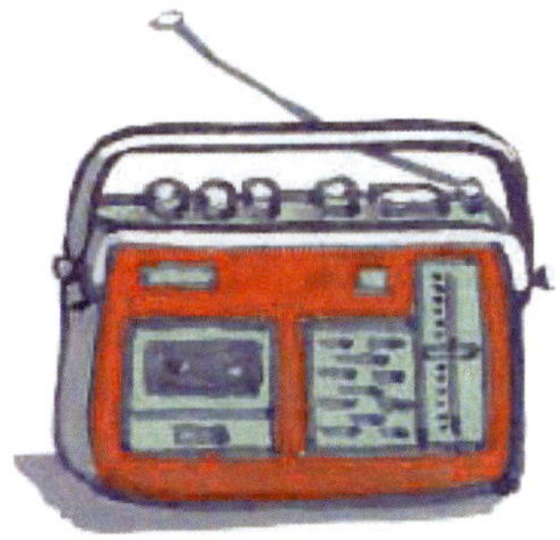

## Objectives of the millenium for development (OMD)

The conference attended by Mayra and Baruani discussed the objectives of the millennium for development. These are goals fixed by many states and organisation that they pledge to fulfill by 2015: reducing poverty and infant mortality rate, fighting epidemics primarily AIDS, making education accessible to all and ensuring durable development for the planet. Even though these objectives are far from being achieved, there definitely has been a progress in that direction. This has given the government a ground to propose more effective measures and to target newer objectives favourable for the planet and for strengthening human rights till 2030.

“I will marry when I want to”

# MEMORY—Fighting against child marriage

**Name** : Memory Banda

**Born** : towards 1997

**Nationality** : Malawian

Malawi is a small and poor African country, perhaps the poorest in the world. Mozambique, Zambia and Tanzania are its neighboring countries and Tanzania is where Baruani took asylum in a refugee camp. In the east lies a big lake. In the high plateaus surrounded by mountains the ways of subsistence are rare forcing the population to live in the plains in the south of the country.

The inhabitants are grouped in small communities and in each a religious leader ensure that the traditions are followed. However, some of these traditions should not even exist like the one that decides overnight that a little girl has grown up to be married. At 13, Memory said 'No'.

## Adulthood at 13

"Memory, you are now an adult, it is time for you to go to the initiation camp."

"We have talked about it before mama, there is no questioning it."

"Look at your sister, she is younger to you and she already has kids."

"I want to study further and I don't want to marry."

"Your mother is right," reasserts her aunt. "You should go there. You have no respect for the traditions of the community."

"I refuse."

## Initiation camps

The camp... the sound of this word jitters Memory. She cannot forget what happened with her sister when she was only 11 years old. That day Memory wowed to resist at her turn. Today she is 13 years old and her turn to go there. The reaction of the people around her is shocking: she is harrowed by her mother, her aunts, her neighbours – what does she think of herself to give her advice and not obey? She was criticized from all around but Memory stood firm on her decision: she is not going to go to this camp!

In Malawi, a tradition is carried on generation after generation: as soon as a girl attains puberty, she has to go to the initiation camp at the end

of which she will be considered adult. But what exactly will she be initiated to? – To satisfy the desires of her future husband. Everyday an old lady will explain them sexual rituals till the 'special day' comes. A man is chosen and paid by the community to sleep with each girl. What a trauma for these young girls some of whom are kids of only 6 or 7 years old!

## End of freedom

These customs prove to be catastrophic for these young girls. They come back from the camp having contracted AIDS or being

pregnant. They are then forced to marry. This is exactly what happened with Memory's sister: hardly 11 she gave birth to a kid. She who dreamt of studying and becoming a teacher, ended up having three kids one after another.

## I will marry when I want to

This sentence is the title of a poem written by one of her friends. Memory made it her motto.

"I will marry when I want to. My mother cannot force me to marry. My father can't force me to marry. My uncle, my aunt, my brother or my sister, cannot force me to marry. I will marry when I want to. Even if they beat me, even if they throw me out, even if they hurt me, I will marry when I want to. I will marry when I want to, but not before I become a teacher and definitely not before I grow up. I will marry when I want to."

## Changing the Law

Since long, Memory had wanted to become a lawyer to help her community. But how could girls even hope to pursue their studies when they have kids even before they are adults? Whatever little they could learn, they forget

that too. Memory had an idea: she was going to put up posters in her village proposing free classes for young adolescent mothers.

Soon 20 young girls joined her class and she taught them to read and write. Gaining in confidence, the young mothers narrated their life and their difficulties: from yesterday to today, they had to leave school, they were not allowed to meet their families. Completely isolated, some became slaves of their family in law.

Enraged by this situation that all the adults around her seem to have accepted and helped by an association that was fighting against forced marriage, Memory learnt to speak in public and organised meetings and groups…

She also made a proposal to the young mothers: together they would mobilise themselves against child marriage. Fortunately, the religious head, a woman was convinced and supports them. They were not alone in this fight. They collaborate with the associations that had been fighting since a long time to advance the legal age of marriage.

## Law or Custom

They succeeded. In February 2015, the legal age of marriage was advanced for 15 to 18 years. It was a huge progress but a lot was still to be done. It was not enough that a law be voted, it was required to implement it. It takes long to change mentalities! In every community the religious heads had to be convinced, the mothers had to be persuaded and young girls had to be informed. Now those who refused to marry before completing their studies knew that law was on their side. They felt confident to build their life as they wanted.

## Deprived of a childhood

Child marriage is a disaster; particularly for the girls a lot of whom die because they are too young to undergo a pregnancy or child delivery or many of them contract AIDS that spreads further. These kids do not have the right to education, to health or to choose their future. Married too early, they are deprived of their childhood. UNICEF, a United Nations organization devoted to the protection of children, fights for minimum 9 years of primary education for all children.

"It is a child labour who give the world
a lesson of courage, not the brand-sponsored
sports stars or the businessmen and their fortune.
These kids are the real heros"

# CRAIG—Ending child labour

| | |
|---|---|
| **Name** | : Craig Lielburger |
| **Birth** | : 17 December 1982, Ontario, Canada |
| **Nationality** | : Canadian |
| **Book** | : Liberating Kids by Craig Kielburger and Kevin Major |

In Canada, a young boy of 12 happily pursued his studies. One morning in April 1995, Craig got ready to go to school. He still had a few minutes and opened the newspaper, The Toronto Star, looking for his comic strips. But a photo and headline on the first page caught his attention. The article that he fell upon changed his life forever.

## The newspaper

"Iqbal Masih, a slave child, freed at 10 years of age and assassinated at 12."

The article talked about a young Pakistani boy, formerly a slave, who fought to end child labour and to free the kids. The owners of the carpet factory were furious to see their free labour disappear and threatened him. Iqbal was shot and he died on the spot. Was it a stray bullet or revenge of the carpet producers, the mystery remains unresolved?

The young Canadian boy was 12, the same age as Iqbal. The article shook him. He knew nothing about the problem of child labour but he had to do something. Craig went to the library, read articles, met associations dealing with child labour and offered his help. Everywhere the answer was the same, "you are too young, come to meet us after a few years." Well, as no-one wanted him, he was going to act on his own.

## The club of 12-12

Few days later he flashed the article in class:

"I gathered information on this: millions of kids are slaves in the world. We are also kids, we should take action. If some of you want to do something about this, we could make a club to think on this."

11, twelve-year-old kids raised their hands and with Craig, they were 12 thus creating the club of 12-12. They spoke in schools, collected funds, appealed for the boycott of companies employing kids. As time passed, Craig was even more convinced. He wanted to meet the slave kids and know their lives. The most difficult was to convince his parents. Finally, they accepted

and Craig prepared for 7 weeks long tour with Alam, a Pakistani student and a family friend. He would record their journey.

In seven weeks, they covered five countries –Bangladesh, Thailand, India, Nepal and Pakistan. Everywhere he met activists fighting for the rights of kids. By hook or by crook, he succeeded in interrogating a dozen kids -victim of flesh trade in Thailand or working in carpet or lighter factories, in railway stations...in the other countries.

Amongst all the kids he met, four impacted him greatly. He was profoundly touched by their lives and they became his friends for life.

## Munnilal

In a city in the north of India, the police and an advocate get ready to step inside a carpet factory accompanied by Alam and a BBC reporter. They liberated around 20 kids but the owner managed to get away. In the bus that took them back to their village, the kids exclaimed in joy: "We are free! We are free!" they shouted in chorus. During the ride, Craig talked to Munnilal, 8 years, sitting next to him:

"Have you ever been to school?"

"Yes, my parents wanted me to learn to read and write. But when I made a mistake, the teacher hit me with a stick and I left school."

Meanwhile someone came to the village and urged my parents to send me with them saying: he can learn to weave carpet along with his studies; that their son will earn a lot of money.

"But I never got any money. They hit me; look at the scars on my back. When the kids cried for their parents, they burnt them with cigarettes. Thereafter i cried silently in my heart."

"You will soon meet your mother. You will be together again", Craig reassured him.

## Nagashir

A few days later, Alam and Craig visited the rest house where the liberated kids spent a few months to rest and regain their confidence. Crais sat beside Nagashir who also worked in a carpet factory. He came there when he was all of 7. He tried to make his younger brother escape from there; his legs, arms and throat were burnt with a red-hot iron rod. When he came to the center, he did not talk; it took him three weeks to hum a song; today he sang that song to Craig:

*"If you want to live, live with a smile. [...]*
*Life is full of ups and downs,*
*Sometimes thunders, sometimes disasters;*
*But don't shed a tear. [...]*
*Live with a smile."*

## Mohan

In the same center, another kid, Mohan ran from a factory where he worked for 5 years. He was very frank and talked freely. Craig called some journalists to tell them about the problems of child labour. Nagashir and Mohan agreed to talk to the journalists. Mohan narrated the brutalities that the kids suffer; two of them who tried to run away were even killed. The meeting was also attended by the councilors of the Prime Minister of Canada who was on an

official trip to Asia: few days later, the Canadian minister agreed to meet Craig to deal with the issue of child labour during his trip.

## Malliga

After spending a few days in Pakistan, Alam and Craig reached Madras in the south of India. They came across kids doing all kinds of jobs: ragpicking, making bols out of scrap metal, domestic help, a little girl filling sweets in packets 11 hours a day...

But the worst they found was a little girl in a building at the end of a road: 8 year old Malliga sat in the middle of a heap of syringes. Craig sat on the floor and talked to the interpreter:

'Where do these syringes come from? What is the kittle girl doing?'

"The syringes are from the hospitals, from the garbage and from the road. She is collecting plastic."

"But she can be infected with Aids! What if she pricks herself?"

"She is going to wash it, that's it. She is not going to get treated, responded the interpreter."

Craig turned towards the little girl:

"This is very dangerous. Do you take any precaution not to be hurt by the needles?"

"I do get hurt sometimes", said the kid.

Craig could not forget his friends. Two years later, he returned to India and met a few of them. Munnilal was with his family and went to school. Nagashir goes around his

village explaining parents that they should not give their kids to the carpet manufacturers. Mohan was a resident in a middle school. He wanted to join the police to arrest the carpet manufacturers.

## Kids helping each other

"My life is divided in two parts: before Asia and after", he said to a journalist. Its true, after his return Craig was not the same. From then on he devoted his life to bring to light the sufferance of kids and to show that the rich countries are somewhere responsible for this situation. He was supported by his parent and his older brother Marc, who was always besides him.

Craig was 16 years old and four years had gone by since the first meeting of his group. The 12 become a few hundred and with more than a thousand kids, the club turned into an association. 70 percent funds of the association come from the efforts of the kids themselves.

## Today

Continuing with his mission, Craig pursued his studies of law and economics. He realized that the problem of child labour is much bigger: the very reasons that forces them to work at an early age to earn money has to be checked. In Nicaragua, for example, the association has created small scale industries which allows parents to earn enough to not send their kids to work and to send them to school.

### Solidarity among Kids

All over the world, even in the developed countries, millions of kids are victims of exploitation and ill-treatment. Many organisations are fighting to make kids aware of their rights and to get the world to respect their rights–Amnesty International fights to get the International Convention of Children's rights implemented and to stop violation of Human rights. ATD quart Monde has created Tapori, a friendship platform for children of all the countries and of all status, where they can share their experiences through articles or common projects.

# Conclusion

To ensure equality, the world will have to change. This definitely requires laws and associations are doing good work in this direction. But it is not enough. It requires everyone to feel responsible like these 8 kids. They understood the importance of education to be able to choose their future on their own and that they show the way for the others to follow. How full of hope and energy are they!. Whatever be their age, the circumstances of their life, each one, wherever they be, can make a difference by creating awareness, by creating links. Each one, wherever they be, can become an active citizen of a world with better justice and solidarity.

To discover the action of KidsRights, the association that discerns the International Peace Prize for children every year: www.kidsrights.org

To discover the action of Amnesty International: www.amnesty.fr

Canada
Colombia
D. R. Congo
Brazil

Pakistan
India
Philippines
Malawi